**COMING OF AGE IN THE SECOND HALF
OF THE TWENTIETH CENTURY**

COMING OF AGE IN THE SECOND HALF OF THE TWENTIETH CENTURY: THE CASE OF GHANA

D. E. K. AMENUMEY
Professor of History, University of Cape Coast, Cape Coast

An Inaugural Lecture Delivered at the University of Cape Coast on 24th June, 1998

GHANA UNIVERSITIES PRESS
ACCRA
2000

Published for the **University of Cape Coast**
by
Ghana Universities Press
P. O. Box GP 4219
Accra

© D. E. K. Amenumey 2000
ISBN: 9964-3-0263-0

Produced in Ghana
Typesetting by Ghana Universities Press, Accra.
Printing and binding by SuperTrade Complex Limited, Accra

DEDICATION

To the memory of my parents Mr. and Mrs. A. C. E. Amenumey who had taken pride in my career but are not alive to savour this moment.

CONTENTS

Acknowledgement

INTRODUCTION 1

PROBLEMS OF COMING OF AGE 4
    Thesis 4
    Specific Ghana Government Policies in the
        Immediate Post Independence Period 11
    Specific U.S.A Government Policies in the
        Immediate Post Independence Period 16
    Development of Personality Cult and Deification
        of Founding Fathers 20
    Problems of Rapid Turnover of Regimes
    Economic Development Management 24
    The Post World War II Era 27
    The Role of the Military 35

CONCLUSION 37

References 40

ACKNOWLEDGEMENT

I pay tribute to all the people who have contributed to my educational growth. They include the teachers at the A.M.E. Zion School at Keta who provided me with a solid foundation, my tutors at the Zion College, Anloga and Keta who built on that foundation, my lecturers at the Department of History, University College of Ghana from 1958 to 1961 and Professors Dennis Austin and William Tordoff of the University of Manchester who supervised my Ph.D thesis. I also thank my colleagues past and present of the Department of History, University of Cape Coast, (UCC), including Professor Francis Agbodeka the first Professor of History at this University, and the secretaries Mr. S. K. Bentil and Mrs. Josephine G. Acquah who typed the original drafts of most of my articles and books.

INTRODUCTION

You may be wondering what my lecture is all about. I want to provide a clue by recounting an incident that happened at Makerere University (where I started University teaching) in January 1964. A public lecture titled "The Greatest Game on Earth" was advertised. Come the day of the lecture, the auditorium was packed. Those of you who are over thirty-five years old will remember that the early 1960s were the period when the "Women's Liberation" movement began. It was the period of the mini-skirt, burning of brassieres and the assertion that anything a man could do a woman could do better. So, most of the audience expected some talk about free love, sex etc. They ignored the fact that Uganda and East Africa generally is safari or big game territory and that the lecturer was a Professor of Zoology. He proceeded to talk about the elephant. The moral of my story is that since I have been introduced to you as a historian and not sociologist or paediatrician, you should not expect a talk on child rearing or any such matter.

Mr. Chairman! An inaugural lecture normally provides a distillation of the essence of an academic's output − a record of his contribution to knowledge and the opportunity to publicize the deep insights he may have developed in his special area of expertise. My area of specialization is African History.

When I embarked on graduate studies in 1961 at the School of Oriental and African Studies, University of London, I was drawn towards ethno-history − the indepth study of individual ethnic groups. At the time, in 1961 there existed a number of general historical studies of Ghana, Togo, West Africa etc. − without any indepth study of specific peoples and states. Of the five of us University College of Ghana History alumni who went to the School of Oriental and African Studies at the time, John Fynn decided to work on Asante and I on the Ewe. Sammy Tenkorang worked on the Slave Trade, the late Kwame Daaku on Trade and Politics on the Gold Coast in the 17th and 18th centuries, while David Birmingham worked on Angola.

Two friends of mine G. K. Nukunya and C. R. Gaba also embarked on the examination of other aspects of Ewe culture i.e.

Kinship and Marriage among the Anlo and Anlo Traditional Religion respectively. It was, therefore, possible for the three of us to inspire and enrich one another's work. For over 30 years we have maintained this collaboration and have recently, together with other scholars, produced a *Handbook of South East Eweland*.

For my part, I have studied various aspects of Ewe history from the precolonial times to the present. This had resulted in the publication of three books and a score and more of articles in academic journals. I have added to the knowledge base on the history of the Ewe and in the process rebutted and put to sleep a number of myths surrounding various aspects of the Ewe history which had been current in the past. Specifically, I have researched the accession of the Ewe to their present home, the circumstances and date of that event. I have examined the nature of the political system established by the new arrivals and the pattern of relationships both between and among the various Ewe groups and between them and their neighbours. In particular I have examined the relations between the Ewe on the one hand, and Akwamu and Asante on the other. I exploded the myth that all the peoples of present day Ghana were contained within the Asante empire. I have also scrutinized the coming of European rule to the Ewe territory and the political, economic and social consequences of that occurrence. One long term consequence of that event was the partitioning of the Ewe territory into different colonial, political and territorial units. I have examined the Ewe unification movement (from 1914 to 1960) which sought to bring together the people split by the European colonial borders. I have put to rest, hopefully, the propaganda circulated by the French Colonial administration against the movement and documented the role France played in frustrating the realization of Ewe Unification which would have changed the post World War II history of both Ghana and Togo.

I am currently bringing my studies up to date by examining the contribution of the Ewe to the history of Ghana. I am compiling the biographies of some Ewe who were the first in their careers in the annals of Ghana. Some of these are Major Seth Anthony – the first African commissioned officer in the army of the British Empire, Dr. R. E. G. Armattoe, the first internationally acclaimed African scientist, Miss Charity Zormelo the first woman graduate, her sister Mrs. Victoria Gorleku the first woman Prisons Officer, J. W. K. Halley the first Inspector-General of Police, Dr. Ephraim Amu and Mr. Philip Gbeho composers of both the unofficial and official national anthems, Mrs. Esther Nkulenu Ocloo the pioneer woman industrialist, Mrs. Annie Jiagee the first woman High Court Judge, black or white, in the British Commonwealth, Mrs. Dzifa Vormawor, first woman captain of the merchant navy among others. It is on the basis of all these works that I earned my academic progress to the rank of professor.

But it is not my contribution to Ewe history that is the subject of my lecture this afternoon. Having subjected the old accounts and image of the Ewe to a critical analysis, I wish to do the same on a broader canvas. Some 23 years ago I published a paper titled "New Myths in the History of Ghana". It has since had the effect of checking the peddling of unfounded claims about aspects of the history of some of the peoples of Ghana.

I believe that a myth surrounds the record of the performance of Africa after independence also. This is an issue that has exercised my mind for some time now. For political reasons some African academics and politicians also peddle this myth. In April 1990 I chaired in this very hall a lecture by an East German friend of mine, Research Professor Peter Sebald from the Academy of Science of the G.D.R. His talk was on the political developments occurring in Eastern Europe at the time, following President Gorbachev's *Glasnost* and *Perestroika*. I predicted that once the imperial hold of Russia was removed, society in Eastern Europe would experience the same growing up pains that had been suffered by post independence Africa which might lead to instability, attempts at secession, repressive regimes and attempts to overthrow them, economic distortion among others. He disagreed with me – implying that some problems were peculiarly African and, white people, whether Eastern or Western, could not be subjected to them. I am quite confident that, being the academic that he is, he will accept that events in Poland, Roumania, Czechoslovakia, former Yugoslavia and what remains of Russia since 1990, have proved me right in characterizing these problems as growing up pains of all societies emerging from colonial, and therefore, by definition, non democratic and exploitative systems, and have nothing to do with racial traits.

PROBLEMS OF COMING OF AGE

I want to focus on the first twenty-five years or so of the history of Ghana — 1957 to 1982 as symptomatic of the problems of coming of age which were and are still being experienced by the newly independent states. This explains the choice of the title of my lecture. The pre-independence antecedents of these states, the milieu into which they were born (or outdoored) and operate in all have a significant bearing on their performance. Above all, the international climate of the post World War II also imposed certain parameters and constraints within which the growing up of these states occurred.

Most observers and commentators assert that the newly emergent Third World countries have not done as well as they were expected to. Opponents of various Third World governments both within and without have continually harped on the shortcomings of the governments concerned. But it seems to me that the problems of coming of age particularly during the second half of the twentieth century have not been fully appreciated by most commentators. By the nature of things, some of these problems are quite different from those faced by the first New Nation — the one that is held to be the yardstick by which success or otherwise had been measured. In other respects, however, the policies and solutions to some of the problems of creating a new stable and viable nation — adopted by the U.S.A. in its formative period were similar to ones being pursued by present day post independence countries. Because Western European nation states had been created quite some time ago, most analysts of these societies have forgotten or conveniently ignore the agonies of the growing pains that some of these European societies went through. Similar or comparable experiences by Third World countries in Latin America, Asia and particularly Africa which attained independence relatively recently in the 19th and 20th centuries, are projected as *sui generis* rather than generic. In other words, these problems are considered to be peculiar to the Third World and particularly African experiences rather than as something which is normative. What has happened since 1990 in what used to be the Soviet Empire should now convince everybody that such developments have to do with the material situation on the ground, to wit – a new society or state emerging out of colonial and by definition, non-democratic, authoritarian foreign rule and nothing to do with the race of the peoples involved.

It is true that some African leaders since independence – civilian and military – have been outright blood-thirsty criminals, some have been tyrants, others crooks, and yet others down right corrupt or incompetent but all this does not negate or diminish the peculiar problems that confront new nations in their attempts to create viable and properly integrated societies out of the disparate units haphazardly brought together in individual colonial territories.

Thesis

I propose to examine the thesis that, given the circumstances in which the newly emergent nations in Africa found themselves, they could not have performed much better that they did from two perspectives:

1. their performance in comparison with the formative years of the U.S.A. — the socalled first New Nation in the late 18th century and

2. from the point of view of the imperatives of the post World War II situation in which the African countries have had to find their feet.

It is my contention that some basic natural laws of progression apply even to organisms such as states. Even the fastest human being has had to crawl and walk before starting to run. Admittedly the duration of each phase of transition varies but the sequence is unalterable. Furthermore, the circumstances of a child's birth do influence the growth and general pattern of development of the particular child. If it is born into a poor home it stands a very good chance of developing *kwashiorkor*. If the child had not been actually planned for, it may lack the devoted parental nurturing that it requires in its formative years. Again, if the circumstance of its birth is such that it becomes an orphan or it is abandoned by its parents, it may face a very bleak future unless a fairy God mother or a foster parent adopts it. The former colonies of Portugal and Belgium fit these last two scenarios respectively.

To take another analogy, if a child is made to choose between a mother and father who are mutually hostile and who demand the exclusive loyalty of that child and continually denounce the other parent, the development of the child into a properly balanced and integrated individual would be stunted or at the worst impaired. This competition for the exclusive loyalty of our putative child could be between a biological parent and a foster parent. Here again the attempts by both the capitalist Western powers and communist Russia to control the affairs of the new states are apposite.

Again, the traditions and heritage bequeathed by the progenitor of the child would influence its behaviour and reaction to varying circumstances. A child brought up in a home where consultation in decision-making is absent would grow to consider that pattern of behaviour to be normative. It would take a strong and robust will on the part of the child to cultivate an attitude of give and take. In this respect also the colonial milieu — the immediate experience of the leaders of the new states under colonial rule would inform their practice after independence.

These scenarios that I have posited by way of illustration are not too far fetched or unrealistic. They actually document the empirical experience of a number of new states in the 20th century.

To look at our problems from another perspective, when one considers the post independence history of Africa as reflective of the African's ability, one should not lose sight of what had been achieved in the long pre-colonial period before the late 19th century. In this regard it should be emphasized that nation building is not a new phenomenon or concept altogether in the African experience. Nations had been created and sustained in Africa well before their counterparts in Europe were created. It is worth reminding ourselves in this context that the process of nation building seriously began in Europe only in the 14th century, by which time many nation-states had already developed in Africa. In what were known as the Western and Central Sudan, the nations and empires of Ghana and Bornu began to emerge well before the end of the first millennium AD, i.e. in the 8th or 9th centuries. The Yoruba and Bini nations of present day Nigeria which are dated to the early centuries of this millennium are also worth citing.

Nearer home, in the 14th and 15th centuries, the Mole-Dagbane states of Mamprugu, Dagbon and Nanung and the Mossi states of present day Burkina Faso were founded. They were all still in existence on the eve of colonialism as was Gonja which had been founded during the 16th century. Asante was founded towards the end of the 17th century and continued to exist till it was colonized. The Fon state of Dahomey (present day Republic of Benin) a contemporary of Asante also remained vibrant for centuries. There are examples from other parts of Africa, like the Solomonid state of Abyssinia.

Most of these political systems remained viable entities for long periods — running into centuries in some cases. In most parts of Africa, the natural and gradual process of state formation and aggregation and legitimization was rudely disturbed and shattered by colonialism from the last quarter of the 19th century. In its place were created new colonial states with ethnic, linguistic, cultural, political and economic components that lacked both rhyme and rhythm. These new territorial units were given artificial boundaries without reference to prevailing conditions and existing political, geographical, ethnic or linguistic ties. These states were held together by the force of the various colonial powers Colonial rule as was established and maintained was essentially non-democratic It was not dedicated to promoting the essential interests of the colonial subjects politically, economically or socially. Whatever benefits the subject people derived were incidental and unintended

In the words of Crawford Young

> the present African states were created through imperial conquest. The structural flaws of the African state system, its fragmentation, illogical boundaries, high cultural pluralism and inherently problematic state-civil society ties derive from this fundamental historical determinant.[1]

After independence, the new leaders of these states were left the task of building or establishing the legitimate right to hold or keep together the various constituent of the state and make nations out of them. No where in Africa did a complete nation emerge out of colonialism. Even in Somalia which is almost completely uni-ethnic, the colonial division into French, Italian and British spheres which was thinly papered over at independence with one state has now resurfaced with a tragic vengeance as demonstrated by the inter clan fighting of the past few years.

The issue to ponder is this! If Africans who had created successful and viable nations, even before Europe started to experiment with that concept, are now making heavy weather of forging nations out of the post colonial states, should not one look for the explanation in what happened under colonial rule and also the conditions of the post independence era — that is the second half of the twentieth century rather than any alleged intrinsic traits or failings of the African? This is one of the important premises of the present discussion.

We shall start our examination with a quick survey of the popular characterization of the post independence record in Africa. The Spring 1982 volume of *DAEDALUS, The Journal of the American Academy of Arts and Sciences* was devoted to examining "Black Africa: A Generation after independence".[2] A number of scholars contributed papers on various aspects of the African post independence experience.

Next in 1984 a number of specialists in African studies were invited to a conference at the University of Indiana. The aim of that conference was to look at Africa 100 years after the Berlin Conference – in particular focusing upon Africa 25 years after independence. A collection of essays which grew out of the lectures and the debates that followed them, edited by G. M. Carter and Patrick O'meara was published by Indiana University Press in 1985[3] and in 1991 the Royal African Society of Britain published the book *Africa 30 years on, the Record and the outlook after thirty years of Independence examined for the Royal African Society.*[4] These three works and a host of other books, articles, papers published since then, on various aspects of the history of post independence Africa are highly critical. Some individual contributors to the three volumes demonstrate some empathy and understanding – an appreciation of the peculiar problems – but nearly all the authors believe that the African states could have done better. Within Africa itself critics and opponents of the various governments have been even more vehement in their denunciation of the "failure" of the regimes in power.

In the words of Peter Calvocoressi:

> Independent Africa is not a success story. Quite the contrary. It has become a byword for incompetent government, political instability, economic disasters, dwarfing the good will and good efforts which have persisted in the face of bad fortune, bad management and bad luck.[5]

Again, Jackson and Rosberg write.

> Since independence the empirical conditions of many subsaharan states have not developed substantially and have deteriorated in some cases. Africa contains the world's largest number of refugees. Genocide has occurred in at least one country Burundi, [of course that has since been overshadowed by a worse one in Rwanda] and ethnic massacres have shaken Rwanda and Uganda. Serious (sometimes violent) ethnic strife has erupted in many countries and political discrimination based on ethnicity has been widespread. By 1983 there had been at least 50 successful coup attempts and major plots.
> Civil wars have been waged in Angola, Chad, Ethiopia, Nigeria, Sudan and Zaire and serious internal conflicts just short of war have shadowed the political life of many other countries. Dictatorship has not been uncommon and in at least two cases, Uganda and Equatorial Guinea, vast numbers of people suffered political abuse and often physical deprivation before the dictators Idi Amin and Francisco Marcias Nguema were over-thrown.[6]

One could add the examples of Emperor Bokassa of Central Africa Republic and Hastings Banda of Malawi.
Jackson and Rosberg state further that

> the economic performance of subsaharan government has generally been poor, and the socio-economic conditions of some countries have been adversely affected, for example Ghana, Uganda and Tanzania. Corruption has become part of the structure of African politics and in some countries for example Ghana, Liberia, Nigeria, is virtual way of life.[7]

In the preface to *African Independence: the First 25 years*, Cater and O'meara (1985: xi) state.

Despite vast amounts in aid between 1962 and 1978 the African continent was in a worsening economic situation as the 1980s began. Population growth continues to outpace food production partly due to persistent drought and a languishing rural economy. Foreign exchange reserves continue to diminish while debts continue to rise. Today (1985) Africa has a high incidence of unemployment and increasing poverty while a tiny proportion of the population accumulates great wealth derived in large measure from patronage and manipulation of political authority.[8]

Specific weaknesses identified by most writers were in the area of political integration, recognized methods of accession to political office, agriculture, industrialization, economic development, freedom of speech and human rights among many others.

On the question of performance in agriculture Lofchie's verdict was that

> After 25 years of independence it has become quite clear that Africa's agricultural sector is not developing. In many countries agricultural stagnation is so pronounced that it poses fundamental constraints on the possibility of development in other spheres of economic life . . . . There is serious and deepening agrarian malaise, the most visible symptom of this malaise is declining per capita food production.[9]

Lofchie states that Africa's population grew at approximately three per cent per annum while its food production remained at two per cent during the 1960s and 1970s. As a result, by the end of the 1970's, per capita food production was only about 80 per cent of what it had been in 1961. This situation forced African states to import food which in turn put a heavy strain on scarce foreign exchange. Very adverse consequences followed. Money that would otherwise have been spent to import other important items needed for long term development including capital goods, spare parts, raw materials and crude oil was used to import food. Consequently, imports which could have increased employment, raised per capital production and improved the general quality of life and also increased the revenue of important government services, were displaced.

Industrialization in Africa has also been faulted. It has been suggested that African leaders put undue emphasis on industrialization as the gate-way to modernization and wealth. The new states aimed at redressing the imbalance between a few advanced industrialized states and the rest of the world through industrial modernization. It was assumed that it was the selfishness of the colonial powers that had kept the colonies economically backward, so once independence had been attained, economic development must quicken. But twenty years after independence, it had become clear that such an analysis was mistaken.

Specific Ghana Government Policies in the Immediate Post Independence Period

These are but a few of the general comments frequently made about independent Africa as a whole. In line with our argument that some of the policies and actions undertaken by independent African states derive from their status as ex-colonies, we shall now examine specific policies and measures undertaken by the government of Ghana in the immediate post independence period and see how they compare with those of the U.S.A. in its formative years.

In 1963 when Ghana was barely six years old and there were 25 other newly independent states existing in Africa, S. M. Lipset published a book titled *The First New Nation. The U.S. in Historical and Comparative Perspective*.[10] In it the author demonstrated to Americans and other critics of the newly independent states, some similarities between the experience of the infant United States and the new African States. I shall expand on Lipset's observations and add other parameters for my exposition. During the first 25 years of independence, Ghana was ruled by six or if you like seven regimes which were alternatively civilian or military, socialist or capitalist orientated, democratically elected or self appointed. There were the government of Kwame Nkrumah and the Convention People's Party 1957 to 1966, the National Liberation Council regime under General Ankrah and Affrifah from February 1966 to September 1969, Dr. K. A. Busia and the Progress Party government from September 1969 to January 1972, the National Redemption Council regime under Col. I. K. Acheampong, January 1972 to 1975, renamed Supreme Military Council, 1, 1975 to July 1978, Supreme Military Council II, under General F. W. K. Akuffo, July 1978 to June 1979, the Armed Forces Revolutionary Council under Flt. Lt. J. J. Rawlings, June to September 1979, Dr. Hilla Limann and the Peoples National Party from September 1979 to December 1981.

In terms of policies pursued and achievements recorded, the differences between the various regimes was one of degree not of kind. The practice of government did not differ very much from one regime to the other. The more noticeable features of government during the 25-year period were – abuse of human rights, particularly under Nkrumah and the various military regimes, state intervention in economic development, low economic performance, low productivity in the face of rapid population growth, unconstitutional rule and frequent changes in government. We shall look at the record of each of these regimes in turn.

The Nkrumah Regime
Nkrumah, the first ruler, has been faulted for being anti-democratic, for introducing the Preventive Detention Act, imprisoning his political opponents, proscribing other political parties and turning the country into a single party state, negating freedom of expression and turning Parliament into a mere rubber stamp. I propose to examine some of these deeds or misdeeds in some detail.

In July 1957, four months after independence, Nkrumah passed the Deportation Act. The first people deported under that law were two brothers who were amongst the most important members of the opposition in Kumasi, a number of Syrians and Lebanese who also supported the opposition parties. Later, that same year in December the government introduced the Avoidance of Discrimination Act. The act banned all organizations, parties and societies which were limited to "particular tribal, regional groups which were used for political purposes". The law made all the existing parties opposed to Nkrumah illegal. These came together to form the United Party.

Government next introduced the Emergency Powers Act which gave it powers to deal more firmly with instances of unrest and disturbance in the country. This law was applied to Kumasi in January 1958. In July, the government passed the Preventive Detention Act. This gave powers to the government to arrest and detain for five years anybody "suspected or found to be acting in a manner prejudicial to the defence of Ghana, to her relations with other states and to state security". The law enabled the government to check the spread of the opposition and deal with persons suspected of threatening state security. From 1958 to 1960 2,000 persons — critics of Nkrumah and those suspected of plotting against him were detained. According to F. K. Buah, as a result of these measures the C.P.P. government strengthened its position and established some peace, order and stability throughout the country. It almost completely destroyed the opposition both in parliament and throughout the country. Of the 32 Members of Parliament in opposition at independence in 1957 by 1960, three were in detention, one in exile and 12 had gone to join the government. Outside parliament, a feeling of fear and insecurity began to grow because of the detentions.[11]

In March 1960, a Republican Constitution was introduced which established the dominance of the President — Nkrumah over other institutions of government. In theory, the constitution recognized the principle of separation of powers between the Legislature, Executive and Judiciary. But even though parliament was described as the supreme and legislative authority, yet article 55 of the constitution conferred special legislative powers on Nkrumah as the first president.[12] He was, therefore, able to make laws by legislative instruments without prior consultation or subsequent approval by parliament. He was also given an absolute veto over parliament. Nkrumah also controlled the election of members of parliament through the constitutional provision that demanded that a parliamentary candidate had to be endorsed by or be acceptable to the Presidential candidate.

In 1964, Ghana was made a one-party state. A plebiscite was held to approve the proposition and also to decide whether the President should have the power to dismiss judges of the High Court at any time for reasons that he considered sufficient. The voting was rigged in favour of the proposal and the C.P.P. became the only party recognized in the country. All other parties became unlawful political organizations. An amendment subsequently empowered the party to recall any Member of Parliament who had become a *persona non grata* to the party hierarchy. In effect parliament met only to endorse and approve the government's decision which actually meant Nkrumah's decisions. When a Member of Parliament, Iddrissu, criticized the government he was dismissed from parliament. Nkrumah was in practice the government.

From 1960 all appointments and promotions to the higher ranks of the Public Service were done by Nkrumah and not the

Public Service Commission. Nkrumah curtailed freedom of the press and closed down newspapers. As he became more and more dictatorial, opposition to him increased and attempts were made to assassinate him. He in turn detained an increasing number of persons, while many fled into exile. Leading politicians like Dr. J. B. Danquah and Mr. Obetsebi Lamptey — former colleagues in the United Gold Coast Convention (U.G.C.C.) and the Big Six died in Nkrumah's preventive detention in 1965.

Nkrumah and his supporters and apologists justified the measure he introduced and applied as being necessary because of plots, sabotage, subversion and the threat of foreign intervention.[13] A government White Paper argued that "the strains experienced by an emergent country immediately after independence are certainly as great, if not greater than the strains experienced by a developed country in war time".[14] David Apter pointed out that indeed "New Nations are plagued with almost the entire range of political problems known to man".[15]

What needs to be stressed is that when Ghana became independent it was far from constituting a nation. British Togoland had been merged with it only on the day of independence. There existed a number of parties and organizations which were based on either ethnic, regional or religious grounds. The general elections held prior to independence had shown that even though the C.P.P. had an overall majority countrywide, yet it was weak in four regions namely, Asante, Volta, Northern and Upper regions. At the actual time of independence further opposition to Nkrumah's government broke out in the form of an uprising in Southern Togoland and the creation of the Ga Shifimokpee, Ga Standfast Association. Buah had argued that Nkrumah feared that if Ghana, the first black African state to regain independence, did not succeed that would affect the fortunes of other territories still under colonial rule. He, therefore, took steps to strengthen his own position and that of his government and remove all obstacles that stood in the path of success.

In varying degrees these harsh methods of dealing with opponents were followed by his successors. There was harassment of political opponents both by judicial means and by security agents under subsequent civilian regimes; and under military governments which were non-constitutional, there were many arrests and detentions and trial by kangaroo courts.

The Busia Regime

When Dr. Busia came to power in September 1969 he summarily terminated the appointment of 568 public servants by misapplying a clause in the new constitution which in spirit sought to provide for continued tenure of office by all public servants from the old to the new regime. He refused to abide by a Supreme Court decision in favour of one of the dismissed public servants, E. K. Sallah, who had taken the matter to court. Again, under a certificate of urgency Busia's government passed at one 17-hour sitting of parliament, a bill banning the selling and public display of Nkrumah's photograph and made the mere mention of his name a criminal offence. Buah calls this piece of legislation "unique in all democratic and civilised nations".[16] Again under Busia, an Industrial Relations Bill was passed in September, 1971 under a certificate of urgency by 68 votes to 28 to abolish the Trades Union Congress.

The Acheampong Regime

Under Acheampong, who toppled Busia in January 1972, a Protective Detention decree was used indiscriminately to intimidate civilians who opposed the policies of his government. Arrest and trials of alleged coup plotters took place. Four coups or plots were alleged to have been hatched against the regime in July 1972, October 1973 and October and December 1975. The alleged plotters were tried but in nearly all cases the penalty of death that was pronounced was committed to long prison sentences. Again in April and May 1978 all prominent leaders of opposition to Acheampong were detained. They included venerable old politicians such as William Offori Atta, K. A. Gbedema and Victor Owusu, as well as younger ones like E. D. Kom, Sam Okudzeto and Adu Boahen.

The AFRC Regime

The Armed Forces Revolutionary Council (A.F.R.C.) short-lived regime (June to September 1979) executed eight top Army Officers including three former Heads of States. Other officers and civilians were tried and given long prison sentences. The regime applied ruthless methods such as whipping of culprits in public, summary dismissals of public officers, confiscation of assets and property by the state and heavy prison sentences in an attempt to root out corruption and commercial malpractices which had crippled the country's economy.

The Limann Regime

The next Head of State, Limann, unceremoniously retired from the army, six top officers including the Chief of Defence Staff, the Head of the Army, Flt. Lt. Rawlings, the former leader of the A.F.R.C., within one month of his assumption of office in September 1979. Throughout 1980 and 1981 Limann's government harassed soldiers — both officers and other ranks — who had been in any way associated with the A.F.R.C. Many were arrested and detained for months without trial while others were dismissed. Rawlings himself, his friends and associates were persecuted by the security agencies over a long period.[17]

Specific U.S.A. Government Policies in the Immediate Post-Independence Period

It is remarkable that the United States also adopted, at independence, harsh laws which aimed at dealing with political dissent or opposition and ensuring unity and stability. The U.S. at independence had fewer disabilities than new states of the twentieth century. Many of the internal conditions that hamper the evolution of stable authority and a unifying sense of national identity in the new states of the twentieth century were much less acute in the early U.S.[18] Yet the evidence suggests that despite its advantages, the U.S. came very close to failing in its effort to establish a unified legitimate authority. The effort was endangered by frequent threats of secession and open flaunting of central authority until the civil war in the next century.[19]

The first twenty-five years of the independent U.S.A. were marked by the presidency of George Washington 1789–1797, John Adams 1797–1801, Thomas Jefferson 1801–1809 and James Madison 1809–1817. During Washington's administration, political division began to emerge on the basis of differences of position with regard to the constitution, financial issues and foreign policy, particularly the relationship with revolutionary France. Because Washington had supported the federal constitution of the new state, people who supported the policies of his administration were called Federalists. His opponents called themselves Republicans. By and large, membership of the two political groups tended to be based on economic, regional and ethnic affiliations of the white population. For the benefit of persons who have no background in American history, the period 1789–1801, that is the first twelve years after independence is called the Federalist era and Thomas Jefferson's Presidency from 1801 is reckoned to mark the inauguration of Republican rule.

Under both the Federalists and Republicans, the U.S. also exhibited problems associated with the coming out of a colonial situation. The record of the U.S.A. during its formative years was quite different from the image that has been cultivated for it as the home of democracy, free speech and the 5th Amendment which specified that "no person shall be deprived of life, liberty or property without due process of law". As James Morton Smith has shown, the Federalists made the U.S. Congress pass a number of Acts in 1789 directed against aliens and political criticism and sedition. These were the Nationalization Act and the Aliens and Sedition Laws. The passing of these laws was the result of a move directed against domestic dissension rather than foreign danger.[20]

The background to all this was that naturalization had been the gateway for immigrants to political participation. The Democratic Republicans – the party in opposition at the time of the Federal era had long attracted the majority of the foreign vote. Due to this, the Federalists hoped to deprive foreign born citizens of their right to engage in political activity. Because they were unable to wholly prevent the Democratic Republicans from recruiting former aliens into their ranks, the Federalists slowed down the process of enlistment by nearly tripling the time required to become a citizen. The Nationalization Act of 1798 lengthened the residence requirement from five to fourteen years for foreigners seeking naturalization as citizens. It was a political manoeuvre by the Federalists designed to cut off an increasingly important source of Republican strength. The Act also subjected all white aliens to a system of national surveillance.

The Aliens Act which was also passed at the same time empowered the President to deport any aliens considered dangerous to the public peace or suspected of treasonable or secret tendencies. And even though the First Amendment to the U.S. Constitution, ratified in 1791, had forbidden Congress to make any law "abridging the freedom of speech or the press", The Sedition Act of 14th July, 1798 prescribed a fine of $2,000.00 and two years imprisonment for any person who should publish any false, scandalous and malicious writings against the government or should stir up sedition in the U.S. As has been pointed out, this was nine years to the day of the storming of the Bastille in France which event was supposed to inaugurate the new liberal attitude throughout the Western World. In the words of J. M. Smith, the evidence is conclusive that the sedition law, as enforced, reduced the limits of freedom of speech and the press in the U.S. to those set by the English common law in the days before the American revolution.[21]

According to Lipset it was quite obvious that the law was designed for partisan purposes. All persons arrested and convicted under it were Republican.[22] Basically Federalist officials and federalist juries enforced the law against their political opponents. All told, Federalist judges jailed and fined 70 persons mostly opposition editors.[23] With few exceptions the trials were travesties of justice, dominated by judges who saw treason behind every expression of Republican sentiments. Grand juries for bringing in the indictments and trial judges for rendering the monotonous verdicts of guilty were handpicked by Federalist U.S. Marshalls in defiance of statutes prescribing orderly procedure.[24]

Federalists not only persecuted Republican editors but on a number of occasions Federalist mobs wrecked Jeffersonian papers and printing presses and beat up their editors. Historians believe that these attempts to undermine democratic rights gave Thomas Jefferson and James Madison a major issue which played an important role in their defeat of the Federalists in 1800.

When Jefferson's Republican party came into office 1801 it proceeded to roll back or modify these laws! In the area of personal liberties, the Republicans sought to eliminate the "despotic legislation" of 1798, as Jefferson called it, by permitting the limited term of the Alien and Sedition Acts to run out without enforcing them, by repealing the naturalization law and replacing it with its more liberal earlier version, and by executive pardons and congressional remission of fines for victims of the sedition statute.[25] Lipset cites Leonard Levy who concluded his survey of freedom of speech and the press in early American history by arguing that the Republicans like the Federalists did not believe in these freedoms when confronted with serious opposition. Each was prepared to use principled libertarian arguments when his ox was being gored.[26] This was similar to what K. A. Busia did in opposition to the C.P.P. government only to demonstrate in 1969–71 that he was no more tolerant of opposition than those people whom he criticized when he was not in government. He also removed the Editor of a government newspaper, the *Daily Graphic,* from his post because he opposed the dismissal of public servants.

Lipset further argues that the various efforts by both Federalists and Democratic Republicans to repress the rights of their opponents clearly indicate that in many ways the early U.S. political officers resembled those heading new states in the twentieth century who view criticisms of themselves as tantamount to an attack on the state itself. Such behaviour characterized leaders of polities in which the concept of democratic succession to office has not been institutionalized.[27]

In this connection the experience of another Western country in creating a new state is apposite and merits a few lines. In France, the Declaration of the Rights of Man and the Citizen adopted by the National Assembly on 22nd August 1789 at the start of the French Revolution stated that:

> the free communication of ideas and opinion is one of the most precious of the rights of man. Every citizen then can freely speak, write and print subject to responsibility for the abuse of this freedom in cases determined by law.

But three and a half years later when war had begun on 29 March 1793 the National Convention adopted a decree on the press to the effect that:

> whoever shall be convicted of having composed or printed works or writings which incited the dissolution of the national representation, the reestablishment of monarchy or any other power which constitutes an attack upon the sovereignty of the people shall be arraigned before the extraordinary tribunal and punished with death.

Both the French decree of 1793 and the American sedition law of 1798 were directed against domestic opposition and reflected a fear of subversion or overthrow.[28] They were no different from Nkrumah's laws. What such laws demonstrate is the tendency of rulers of new states or post-revolutionary regimes to wish to cow all opposition to themselves as a means to ensuring stability and the ultimate survival of their own rule which they confuse with the survival of the state itself.

Development of the Personality Cult and Deification of Founding Fathers

The next common feature we want to examine is the development of the personality cult and deification of founding fathers. There has been a lot of criticism of the personality cult that characterized Nkrumah's regime – the decision to put his image on the national currency, the naming of numerous institutions, avenues after him, the erection of his statue in front to Parliament House, the recital by the Young Pioneers of "Nkrumah never dies", the grandiose appellations that were recited at state functions he attended etc.

Here again one can identify a comparable development in George Washington's U.S.A. As Lipset has pointed out, one basic problem faced by all new nations and post revolutionary societies is the "the crisis of legitimacy" – i.e. "to whom is loyalty owed and why"? The fastest and easiest way to resolve this problem is to exploit the charisma of the new leader or head of the state.

> Legitimacy of any kind is derived from shared beliefs, that is, from a consensus as to what constitutes proper allegiance; such a consensus develops slowly. Where traditional legitimacy is absent as it was in Post revolutionary America or France, or in much of contemporary Africa and Asia, it can be developed only through reliance on legal or charismatic authority. Charismatic authority is well suited to the needs of newly developing nations. It requires neither time nor a rational set of rules and is highly flexible. Charismatic authority can be seen as a mechanism of transition, an interim measure which gets people to observe the requirements of the nation out of affection for the leader until they eventually learn to do so out of loyalty to the collectivity.
> The early American republic like many of the new nations was legitimized by charisma. In his time George Washington was idolized as much as many of contemporary (1960s) leaders of new states.[30]

To demonstrate this fact, Lipset quotes the observation of a French visitor to the U.S., Paul Svinin, in 1815 who reported that "Every American considers it his sacred duty to have a likeness of Washington in his home, just as we have the image of God's saints. Babies were being christened after him as early as 1775 and while he was still President his countrymen paid to see him in waxwork effigy".[31] But a phenomenon that was comparable in nascent Ghana and other parts of Africa was condemned and ridiculed by most American and Western commentators who conveniently forgot about their own past.

Problem of Rapid Turnover of Regimes

Another feature of the history of Ghana after independence has been the rapid and often unconstitutional change in government and the attendant turmoil, discontinuity, instability and the prevention of democratic institutions from taking root. We shall come back to military intervention specifically later on. For now we shall discuss the general problem of rapid turnover of regimes. As indicated earlier, between 1957 and 1982, Ghana lived under seven regimes. A number of reasons have been suggested for this high frequency of change. These have to do with the wholesale adoption at independence of an alien political system that had not developed any roots historically in the country and the consequent lack of any genuine commitment to it and attempts by Nkrumah to perpetuate himself and the C.P.P. in power, thereby foreclosing all possible avenues of legitimate and constitutional transfer of power. There was also the tendency on the part of governments to disregard the opposition and alternatively the attitude of the opposition to oppose all and every government measure without any reference to its merit. Other reasons were the incompetence, corruption and abuse of power by persons in authority – either in government or the public service, the politicization of the Armed Forces and the personal and group ambitions of some members of the Forces.

Even if the U.S.A. did not undergo any seizure of power by the Military it also experienced the instability which was the result of the problems of getting a new legal-political system and all its implications accepted by everybody within the state. As pointed out by Lipset, one of the pre-conditions for ensuring a stable democratic state is to establish a clear distinction between the state and the individual government of the day. In the U.S.A. difficulties encountered in achieving this nearly led to the failure to create a nation. It is only when one recognizes this fact that one can appreciate the difficulties faced by the present new nations which have more complex and less favourable circumstances than the U.S.A.[32] Another American author, Cunliffe, has demonstrated that the quality of the period 1789 to 1837, that is the first 48 years after independence, was not tranquil. And that in some respects especially up to 1815 it was a time of prolonged crisis full of regrets and foreboding, hostility and confusion.[33]

Lipset compared the turbulent period 1789 to 1801 when the Federalist Party was in power and tried to use the charismatic power of George Washington to legitimize the new system of authority in the infant U.S.A. with the turmoil experienced in the newly independent Ghana where the government tried to create some measure of legitimacy through the person of its charismatic leader Kwame Nkrumah. He pointed out rightly that the older nations tended to view with impatience the internal turmoil of the new nations and moreover expect these nations to achieve in one decade what other nations took a century and more to achieve. A study of the history of the early U.S.A. would reveal that there is no basis for the notion that the U.S.A. proceeded smoothly and without any problem to establish democratic political institution. During the early period when political legitimacy and party government were being established,

> It was touch and go whether the complex balance of forces would swing in the direction of a one or two party system or even whether the nation would survive as an entity. It took time to institutionalize values, beliefs and practices and there were many incidents that revealed how fragile the commitment to democracy and nationhood really was.[34]

Another charge levelled at governments of newly independent African states including Ghana is that they have failed to achieve national unity or integration. In some African states like Nigeria Sudan, Niger, Chad, Morocco, Angola, Mozambique, Ethiopia and Somalia there have been instances of attempted secession or civil war. In Ghana, at independence, there were attempts to take the former British Togoland out and there were also threats of secession from Asante. Even now, accusations and counter accusations of tribalism testify that integration is not yet complete. But the problem is a big one. This issue of creating a feeling of national unity among diverse elements is one shared by all new nations. In the first place, the political boundaries of the new states are artificial and do not reflect pre-colonial socio-political realities, hence the persistence of parochial attitudes. The problems of national unity and consensus in African and Asian states are more complex than those faced by the U.S. when it became independent of Britain. Many African and Asian states contain many linguistic groups and ethnic units, several of which have histories of bitter antagonism to one another. On the other hand, the U.S. was formed by a relatively homogeneous population (at least those who were allowed to participate in politics) with a common language, relatively similar religious background and a common cultural and political tradition.

Despite this fact and the experience of working and fighting together in a seven year struggle for independence, the best governmental structure which the Americans could devise was a loose federal union under the Articles of Confederation. This union lacked any national executive and in effect preserved most of the sovereignty and authority of each state. There were many threats to secede in the first decade of national existence and the threats came from both the northern and the southern states. In 1798, two future Presidents, Thomas Jefferson and James Madison, sought the passage by a state legislature of nullification ordinances which proclaimed the right of each state to decide the extent of national authority to be tolerated within its boundaries.

As Chambers puts it, the strength of the new national fabric (of the U.S.) was repeatedly tested. After they had left office in 1801, various Federalist leaders (that is of Washington's party) sought in 1804, 1808, 1812 to take the new England (that is the North-Eastern states) or the northern states out of the union.[35] The experience of twentieth century new African states with which we are familiar was no different from that of the U.S. at a similar stage of development.[36] In the early U.S., as in contemporary new states, the achievement of national unity and respect for national authority was no easy task. The possibility of secession remains one of the basic problems facing many new states in our century.

Economic Development Management

Another area of activity in which government policy in Ghana has been faulted is that of economic development — particularly direct state intervention and alleged wrongness of that policy and therefore its failure. According to Rhoda Howard, because Ghana was a colonially created state with little economic independence, the regimes that have held power have pursued essentially the same economic strategy — that is "state intervention in an attempt to effect some structural changes in the direction of agricultural and industrial independence within the framework of continued core capitalist domain".[37]

For Ghana as for other developing countries, the need for economic planning comes from the realization that only when a comprehensive economic policy is implemented can the state accelerate its pace of economic growth. The objective is to raise the standard of living to levels comparable to those of the developed countries. Since resources are limited as compared to the range of the needs of the country, economic policy is aimed at making the maximum use of resources so as to increase goods and services. In this connection, economic planning which produces development plans is adjudged the cheapest means to achieving socio-economic development.

In 1951, when the C.P.P. came into office – that is six years before independence, there were many services which were not sufficiently strong to support a serious development programme. Agricultural services were inadequate to support the agricultural development on a continuing scale. Water supplies, electricity, health and sanitation services were in danger of being overtaken by the growth of the population. Large areas remained isolated from the rest of the country, because of lack of adequate transportation and communication facilities. In the area of social services, primary education reached less than half the children of school-going age. Facilities for secondary and higher education were limited in supplies and shortages existed in the area of preventive medicine and other basic facilities.

It was in such circumstances that Nkrumah introduced a number of development plans to provide or extend these economic and social services with which rapid agricultural and industrial development could be supported. The first development plan was for 1951–57, the second 1959–1964. The first was followed through but the second was scrapped after two years. The third development plan was for seven years, 1963–1970. But it was abandoned with the fall of Nkrumah in 1966. Investment by the state in business enterprises began with the establishment of the Industrial Development Corporation. It was to promote industrial expansion in the country by financial, advisory and technical assistance in the establishment and development of new and existing industries and for the training of local personnel for management purposes. By 1960, there were 55 state owned corporations other than banking and financial industries. Capital invested by the government in these corporations was over £80 million. There were 12 Joint State and private enterprises. Government investment in these joint stock and private corporations was about £1.2 million. Unfortunately the measure of industrial expansion which might have been expected from the number of state corporations was not achieved.

This policy of state investment in the economy has been criticized, but there is logic in its adoption by new nations including those in Africa. In new states, for the people to accept the right of the rulers to govern, the rulers must demonstrate effectiveness which translates into economic development – the provision of economic goods and raising of the peoples' standard of living.

> As most states lack the traditional means of rapid economic growth, they have been led in recent years to introduce large scale government planning and direct state intervention. The desire to use the state to direct and speed up the process of economic growth rests on the dual necessity to demonstrate effectiveness to the various groups within the polity and to display national competence. The leaders seek development as part of their more general effort to overcome feelings of national inferiority particularly *viz a viz* the former metropolitan power.[39]

Similar processes had been at work in the case of the U.S. also.

In the early stages of economic development in the U.S.A., there had been a great deal of government intervention and even public investment in the economy so as to develop industry and commerce.[40] To stimulate economic growth, the federal and the state governments intervened actively in the economy during those years.[41] It was at the state level that most government effort was undertaken. Many states considered it proper and necessary to use public funds to develop transportation facilities, banking, manufacturing etc. The states employed various devices to promote economic growth. Sometimes it was through legislation by the setting up of inspection standards. At times, it was direct encouragement in the form of financial help from lotteries or in bounties. At yet other times, they did so through franchises which were in effect monopolies that protected companies from competition in their infancy. In many states, government invested directly in or owned various companies whose development was considered necessary for economic growth in the public interest.[42]

According to Cunliffe, individual U.S. states entered commerce and industry through the device of the mixed corporation by which state funds were allocated for enterprise to chartered organizations.[43] The states found the granting of charters to new corporations the most successful means of promoting economic development. The most important promotional policy became that of chartering business corporations.[44] Direct government financing of economic activities which required large sums of capital occurred in many states. The story of state and local investment in early economic development in the U.S. clearly justifies the conclusion that government, in this period played a role corresponding to that envisaged in most nations today.[45] The economy of the country was new and undeveloped but large amounts of investment capital were required. This need could only be met internally from government sources since the new states had committed themselves to economic development. Therefore the American political leaders justified state participation in economic activity.

But the U.S. was more fortunate than most ex-colonial countries of today. Besides the assistance from the industrial states, rapid economic growth during the formative period of the U.S. economy benefited from massive foreign capital provided by outside investors, particularly, the British.

The Post World War II Era

So far, we have seen that under comparable circumstances, leaders of new states in the past and at the present have followed policies that were broadly similar. So that George Washington's U.S. and Nkrumah's Ghana, coming out of a colonial situation had only a certain limited set of options. But other imperatives were imposed on the leaders of Ghana by the fact that Ghana had to come of age in the post World War II era. The post World War II period was characterized by a number of realities that dictated the options available to leaders of small states. Some of these imperatives that are pertinent to our study are the cold-war and super-power rivalry, a more heightened awareness of the social responsibilities of government to their people, that is, the obligation to provide social services like shelter, education, medical care and greater regard for human rights. The improved global communication system made people of one state aware of conditions in other states and therefore compare their own local situation to that of others and consequently become less easy to satisfy. On the labour front, it meant a limit on how long citizens could work per day or per week and certain rights that they are entitled to as workers etc. In a period after 1973, the impact of the petrol crisis was another liability. We shall examine the implications of some of these factors.

One of the most important phenomena that adversely affected the efforts of new states during the second half of the twentieth century was the super-power rivalry of the post World War II era. It was the misfortune of the African states, and for that matter many Asian States also, that they acquired their political independence at the time of the global struggle between the U.S. and U.S.S.R. The two Super-Powers regarded the entire world as an arena for their mutual hostilities. One aspect of this rivalry was the ideological competition between capitalism and communism as the only path towards economic prosperity, But as Crowford Young points out,

> the great game has goals that African states found irrelevant, was governed by a logic which they rejected, had rules of conduct which they repudiated yet could not resist the extension of the playing field to in-

clude the nominally independent African continent. Add to this the many stranded fabric of relationships to secondary players in the great game – the former Western European powers and the compelling logic of the impossible obstacles to non-alignment became clear. The African state system is thus placed at continuing risk by the polarising effects of recurrent Great Power crises. The competitive recruitment of friends and allies and the continuing impact of their global competition upon American and Soviet approaches to Africa exacerbated some tensions within Africa and artificially introduced others.[46]

American policy was characterized by a desire to minimize the influence of the U.S.S.R. There tended to be a zero-sum assumption about Russia's relations with Africa. Whatever Russia gained in Africa was considered a loss to America and vice-versa. The determination to pre-empt the Soviet Union led the U.S.A. to commit itself to supporting governments and organizations willing to promote its global interest like limiting the spread of communism. So the U.S.A. supported apartheid South Africa, Zaire, Morocco and Jonas Savimbis UNITA movement in Angola. On the other hand the Soviet Union was also determined to weaken the old links between the New African States and the capitalist countries and generally make things difficult for the latter in Africa. But such global political interest of the World Powers did not serve the real needs of Africa. "Africa did not want to take either side in the cold war, but to get what it could from both".[47]

In the words of Colin Leys,

> The impact of Great Power military and geographical intervention has been important. They may well have been decisive, especially economic and military support for political clients and economic and military intervention against opposing forces, encouraging high levels of military spending and fostering military coups and wars.
> For example, for 28 sub-saharan African countries (excluding South Africa) for which estimates can be made, the real levels of military spending rose four-fold between 1965 and 1972. In 1976, 20 sub-saharan African countries were spending an average of 3.1% of G.D.P. on their armies, not far below the levels of the rich Western European NATO countries. For countries that were among the poorest of the world, these were crippling expenditures. An important part of the expenditure was directly due to imperialist military threats as in post 1974 Mozambique and Angola or was the outcome of complex Great Power manoeuvres as in Ethiopia and Somalia.[48]

This situation imposed certain restrictions on the foreign policy options of new 20th century states as compared with the 18th century U.S.A. The U.S. began life as a unified nation about the time that the then two strong powers, France and Britain had started their conflict that was to last twenty five years. American foreign policy at that time was dictated by national interest, it was essentially expediential. It threatened war at one time or the other with both sides by taking their territories in America – to wit Louisiana, Florida and Canada. The leaders of America took the position that as a new nation with the need to secure a legitimate structure of authority and rapid economic development, they must abstain from involvement in foreign entanglements.[49] George Washington outlined two principles that guided American foreign policy at least until the late 1940 – that is maintain commercial but not political ties with other nations and enter no permanent alliances.[50]

There was a slow accreditation of foreign ambassadors to the U.S. The latter had made satisfactory commercial treaties with France in 1778, Netherlands in 1782, Sweden in 1783, Prussia in 1785, and Morocco. It was only in 1791 that Britain sent a properly accredited minister to the U.S.A. France, which had recognized the independence of the U.S.A. by its 1778 treaty, was also cool towards it. Only after the French revolution broke out in 1789, did the Franco-American link became emotionally stronger.

Until 1793 when Republican France which had been invaded by enemies declared war on Britain, Austria, Prussia, Sardinia and the Netherlands, the U.S.A. had no need for a foreign policy. Now, the U.S. Congress passed a Neutrality Act in 1794 forbidding American citizens to participate in the war and prohibiting the use of American soil as a base of operation for either side. America was able to adhere to this neutrality policy for nearly twenty years. In 1794, the Jay Treaty was signed with Britain. This introduced an improvement in American relations with Britain. The French professed to regard the treaty as a hostile act because the U.S. was still bound to them by the alliance in 1778. In 1795 a treaty was signed with Spain. In 1800, an agreement of commerce was signed between the U.S.A. and France.

In contrast to what the U.S. was able to achieve in the foreign policy arena, Ghana did not enjoy such freedom of operation. Ghana became independent at the height of the Cold War. Russia and the U.S. were competing for influence and control over the rest of the world. At the time there were a few non-western countries in Asia – such as Japan, China, India, Burma and Pakistan and in Latin America and Liberia and Ethiopia in Africa which were independent. Fifty-six nations sent delegates to Ghana's independence celebrations. It was considered necessary to respond to the gesture formally by opening diplomatic missions in some of these countries.

Nkrumah's foreign policy was based on non-alignment or what he called "positive neutrality". Immediately on becoming independent, Ghana applied for membership of the U.N.O. Nkrumah also kept Ghana within the British Commonwealth of Nations and maintained the connection between Ghana and Britain. He next established firm relations with U.S.A., France, Western Germany and Australia. He also established contact with some Soviet bloc countries like U.S.S.R., Poland, Czechoslovakia, East Germany and also with China, India and Israel.[51]

By 1964, Ghana had diplomatic relations with 56 countries. Ministry of Foreign Affairs personnel at January 1964 was 187. Succeeding governments have, on coming to power, reduced the number only to increase it later. For example, after the 1966 coup d'etat, there was a forty per cent reduction of the number of embassies to save costs, but that did not last very long. Today, Ghana has 37 missions and 46 consulates abroad.

While it is true that Ghana has not been reduced to the level of Zaire in not being able to pay its diplomatic staff, there is little doubt that the need to be represented in many foreign countries has cost the country dearly. The need felt by the infant Ghana to open many embassies contrasted with the situation in George Washington's U.S. Apart from Britain from which it had broken away; France which had gone to its aid during the war of independence, Spain which possessed territory adjacent to the U.S. and Holland which had also helped the U.S. financially, there was no pressing need to open embassies elsewhere. On the other hand, the exigencies of the cold-war situation, post World War II, improved global communication and the need to project the image of the first independent black state dictated representation in countries belonging to both the West and East political divide and a select number of non-aligned states in Latin America, Asia and the rest of Africa.

Post World War II Social Imperatives

The eighteenth century government of U.S.A. was not subject to the same kind of pressure to provide social services as new states in the second half of the twentieth century whose citizens expect their government to behave exactly like contemporary well established older polities. When the U.S. became independent, it was one month's distance from Europe and six months from Asia.

> The absence of mass communication systems meant that Americans were relatively isolated, and hence did not immediately compare their conditions with those in the more developed countries. The U.S. did not face a revolution of rising expectations based on the knowledge that life was better elsewhere. The accepted concepts of natural and appropriate rights did not include a justification of the lower classes organised participation in the polity to gain higher incomes, welfare support from the state and the like.[52]

This picture contrasts most vividly with one painted for Ghana in 1976 by P. Kennedy.

> What were luxury goods for one generation tend to become subsistence goods or at least essential commodities for the next. In Ghana today, the government is trying to control the distribution and therefore the price of a number of basic goods precisely because they are in such great demand. Some of these now seem to be regarded as 'essential' goods e.g. washing powder, toilet soap and tinned milk whereas this was not the case twenty years ago. Other commodities too, like transistor radios, bicycles, tooth paste, and possession of good clothes in addition to everyday clothes appear to be widely owned and used in the towns by the poorer section of the community.[53]

That was in 1976, the situation is even more serious today.

It should be immediately obvious that it would be much more difficult for the political leaders of Ghana in the 1970s to meet the economic and social expectation of their people than the leaders of the U.S. in the late 18th century. If we examine the area of education for example, we see the same contrast in pressures and responses.

In the U.S.A., during the early post independence era, several of the states endorsed the principle of public education, but none actually required the establishment of free schools.[54] As late as 1815, that is over 25 years after independence, none of the states within the U.S. had in actual operation a comprehensive public school system. Outside New England (N.E. States), schooling continued to be viewed as the responsibility of the family and the church, rather than the state. In the middle Atlantic region and the south, most schools were run by religious groups, by proprietary school masters i.e. private individual teachers or by philanthropic societies. Even where schools were public, there was no system of universal education.

By 1815, there were a little over 100 private secondary schools in the U.S. of which 67 were in the two states of Massachusetts and New York alone. Again at the outbreak of the revolution, there had been a total of 9 Universities in the U.S. By 1800, the number had risen to 22 of which five were state Universities. The largest of these Universities had an enrolment of no more than a few hundred students and the total endowment of these institutions amounted to little more than $500,000.00. [55]

By contrast, in 1951, when Nkrumah's C.P.P. became associated with government, primary education reached less than half the children of school-going age. Facilities for secondary, technical and higher education, though of high quality were nevertheless limited in supplies. Nkrumah introduced the Accelerated Development Plan for Education which aimed at expanding educational facilities at all levels. Primary education was made fee free in 1952 and compulsory in 1961. By 1960, the proportion of the population with some school education was 21 per cent (50–60 percent in the southern towns, but less that 10 per cent in the north). The number of pupils in the primary schools rose from 144,000 before 1951 to 928,000 in 1963; in the middle schools from 60,000 to 233,000 and in the secondary schools from under 3,000 to 28,000. By 1966, there were three Universities and the Kwame Nkrumah Ideological Institute at Winneba with a total enrolment of 5,000 students. There was the Institute of Adult Education with 10,000 students. Primary and middle schools numbered 9,988 with 1,286,486 pupils and 81 secondary schools with 32,971 students, 47 Teacher Training Colleges and 14 Technical schools. Succeeding regimes after 1966 have uniformly continued to expand the scope of educational services and facilities.[56]

If we turn to labour and working conditions, we again see that demands and expectations in the post World War II period were quite different from those of the 18th century. When the U.S. achieved independence, the relatively long hours that American workers put in in both factory, industry and presumably public service helped to accelerate economic development. For the most part, factory workers worked for between 13 and 16 hours a day.[57] One worker recalled his early years in these words "I worked 15 hours a day. I used to go in at a quarter past four in the morning to work till a quarter past eight at night having 30 minutes for breakfast and the same time for dinner".

A series of strikes led to the acceptance of a ten hour work day for artisans and merchants, but factory hands worked longer days.[58] Long after the 10 hour day became common elsewhere, factory workers still worked for 11 to 13 hours a day. A law passed by the state of Massachusetts in 1841 forbidding the employment of children under the age of 12 for more than 10 hours a day was considered a progressive law indeed.

Again, during the period 1789 to 1815, there was no recognized labour union activity.[59] Employers were opposed to workers' unions because they felt that they were unable to meet the demands of the workers. They turned to the courts system for help. In the courts, workers's societies were attacked as combinations or conspiracies in restraint of trade. Between 1806 and 1842, there were a number of conspiracy trials against labour strikes and joint action to raise wages. Such law suits severely hurt the legal case of the workers. It was only in 1842 that the doctrine of criminal conspiracy was laid to rest. The law in the state of Massachusetts recognized the right to strike. Even then, employers continued to use the courts as weapon against unions until President Roosevelt's New Deal (1933–45).

By way of contrast, at the time that Ghana became independent, the International Labour Organization conventions determined conditions in the work place. The most important of these was the length of the work day and week. At independence, the work week stood at 5½ days for all public servants except teachers. But by 1963, the work week had been cut to five days and forty (40) hours all-told.

Now it may be alright for states that have already been established to demand only so much out of their workers, but for new nations struggling to establish themselves and bridge the gap between themselves and the advanced nations, this is a luxury that is ill-conceived. If society were fully alive to the need for everybody to put his shoulder to the wheel, organized labour itself would see the need for longer working hours in new states, irrespective of what happens in the older ones.

There is, also, the issue of too many public holidays. In Ghana we observe too many holidays. These are new Year' Day. Eid-ul-Fitr, Independence Day, Good Friday, Easter Monday, Eid-ul-Adhar, May Day, June 4th, Republic Day, Farmers' Day, Christmas Day, Boxing Day. In the past, we also celebrated various coup days like 24th February, and 31st December. Till 1996 when some of the statutory holidays fell on Saturday and Sunday, we postponed them to the next working day or days. As if these were not bad enough, organized labour has found ways of wheedling and wangling a few more. On 24th December, 1993 the following circular came from the office of the Acting Deputy Registrar (Administration), U.C.C.

Christmas and New Year Holidays.
It has been decided that the University will break for the Christmas Holidays after 12.30 p.m. and resume work on January 4 1994. This means that the two days within the Christmas and the New Year festivities i.e. 29th and 30th December which should normally have been working days have been added to the holidays with the kind permission of the Vice-Chancellor. Signed . . .

Mr. Chairman, I do not think you should feel bad about this, because I am sure other Chief Executives throughout Ghana also found it necessary to grant this "kind permission". In 1997, the entire period from midday 24th December to January 5th 1998 was declared an extended vacation at the University of Cape Coast. The four regular working days involved were designated "compulsory leave for all staff and may be (not shall be) set against your leave entitlement". I am yet to see any modalities for enforcing this liability. Meanwhile a number of people have already taken the 1998 annual leave. The cumulative effect of all these holidays – statutory and gratuitous is that productivity is affected.

Cuba which has postponed and abolished otherwise fixed holidays like Christmas to complete the harvesting of sugarcane – the life-blood of its economy has shown that new states should be able to decide collectively for themselves what is appropriate in their peculiar national circumstances. The point I am making is that if the leaders of the present new states can be guaranteed the same amount of man hours of work as the older states enjoyed in their formative years, the pace of development would increase appreciably.

The Role of the Military

Another important contrast between the problems faced by Ghana and the U.S. in their respective formative years has been the role of the military. During the first 25 years of Ghana's independence, the armed forces held power for 12 years. The reasons for military intervention have been diverse – selfish, self-serving or altruistic. The soldiers have been either hailed as saviours or condemned as traitors to the constitution. Whatever the motives, military intervention has contributed to instability and untimely changes in government. But if there had been no army, that option of getting rid of governments that a section of the citizens might consider unpopular, or authoritarian or incompetent would not exist.

At independence, Ghana had a military establishment which consisted of a regiment made up of three Infantry Battalions, a field battery of artillery and various supporting units, an Officers Training School at Teshie and a British Royal Signals unit of two officers and 31 other ranks on loan from Britain. By 1956, of the 212 officers in the Gold Coast army, 184 were British and only 28 indigenous. After independence an Air Force and Navy were added and Ghanaianization of the officer corps, was accelerated to match the Ghanaianization of the top hierarchy of the public service.

By 1959, there were 79 Ghanaian officers in the army with

37 officer cadets at Teshie and another 24 in the United Kingdom. In 1959 and 1960, the three ranking Ghanaian officers were promoted from Major to Lt. Colonel and appointed to command the three battalions. In September 1961, the British officers were dismissed. Between 1960 and 1963, 168 new officers were commissioned. By 1965, the total strength of the Army, including President Nkrumah's own Guard Regiment was 14,000 officers and men. In 1967, there were 705 officers in the Army ranging from second Lieutenant to Lieutenant General.[60]

This meant that, as pointed out by Lipset in connection with many contemporary new nations, "there exists a potentially politically powerful military class who have a patriotic national outlook, who may use the army to seize power if it becomes impatient with civilian leadership".[61] This is what happened in 1966, 1972, 1979 and 1981. We may debate whether it was "patriotic national outlook" that inspired these instances of military intervention or not.

But the contrast with the situation in the U.S. is clear. When the U.S. was seeking to establish a national authority. It was not bedevilled by any such class of citizens. The entire army of the U.S. in 1781, consisted of 672 men and even after a decade of threats of war, there were only 3,349 soldiers in 1800. It is true that the potential military strength was much larger for it included various state militia reserves. But the latter were simply the citizenry and so long as the government enjoyed the loyalty of the general population, it had no need to fear its professional soldiers.[62]

It should be clear from what has been said so far that, apart from some common problems which Ghana shared with the 18th century U.S.A., the new Ghana faced conditions which were infinitely more complicated and more difficult than those faced by the First New Nation. In assessing the success or failure of the leaders of independent Ghana, therefore, one should take account of this reality. Any omission to do so would be unhistorical and untenable.

CONCLUSION

To sum up, the purpose of this lecture has not been to excuse or justify the failures and short-comings of independent Africa's first crop of rulers. There is little doubt that some of these have been blood-thirsty tyrants like Marcias Nguema of Equatorial Guinea, Idi Amin Dada of Uganda, Emperor Bokassa of the Central African Republic and Mobutu Sese Seko of Zaire. Others had clung to power long after their period of usefulness like Hastings Banda of Malawi, Kenneth Kaunda of Zambia, David Jawara of the Gambia, Eyadema of Togo. Yet others have been incompetent and ineffectual.

In the specific case of Ghana, some leaders like Nkrumah had been intolerant of opposition and dissent and did everything to perpetuate their rule; others like Busia threw their democratic ideas to the wind once they assumed power. Acheampong was corrupt and incompetent. Limann was overwhelmed by the problems of government and floundered helplessly while others like Rawlings were ruthless and prepared to push the people to their utmost limit of forebearance in the interests of their cherished ideals.

All this is true; nevertheless, generally African leaders have achieved more than they have been given credit for. It should be clear from what I have been saying that the superficial assessment, that is the standard bill of fare, fails to take account of both the intrinsic problems of creating new nations out of colonial territories, and also the additional peculiar conditions of the post World War II era in which new African states have had to establish themselves as viable nations. In the first place, African achievements and successes in nation building before the colonial era are ignored. Secondly, their record in the area of social development after colonial rule is de-emphasized and their "failure" in economic development is stressed. The insinuation is peddled subtly that there must be something deficient or lacking in the African make-up.

It has been argued by some people that 30 years or so after independence, African countries cannot continue to blame their woes on colonialism. Some African commentators who seem to think that it makes them appear sophisticated and objectively learned have also subscribed to this assertion. But what such a view betrays is ignorance of what colonialism was about and why the colonial powers were prepared to concede political independence to Africa. It betrays a lack of the realization that political independence was granted because the colonial powers had woven a network of economic relations that made their continued political rule redundant and pointless, while at the same time guaranteeing their continued economic control over the former colonies. It was no longer necessary to maintain a colonial apparatus to ensure that African states continued to produce raw materials for the industries of their former masters and their friends, and in turn to consume the finished products of those industries, without any control over the prices of either imports or exports. It was this continuing ability of the former colonial powers to dominate the new states as it were by remote control that restricted the later's freedom of action and effectively hamstrung their political independence.

Again, the examples of some Asian countries like Hong Kong, Singapore, Taiwan, Malaysia and South Korea have been cited as success stories that give the lie to African excuses and rationalizations. But here also, what is conveniently ignored is the fact that the circumstances of the "Asian Tigers" were not exactly the same as of most ex-colonies. They did not start from the same base as any Africa ex-colony.

At independence Ghana was the most advanced of the black African states but in terms of a number of factors which are crucial for economic and industrial advance like human resource development and infrastructure it lagged woefully behind these South-East Asian countries. For example, in 1960 the adult literacy rate in Ghana was 27 per cent as contrasted with 71 per cent in South Korea, 53 per cent in Malaya, and 68 per cent in Thailand. In the same year, of the children of school-going age attending primary schools, the figures were 38 per cent for Ghana, 94 per cent for South Korea, 96 per cent for Malaya and 83 per cent for Thailand. The figures for secondary school students were 5 per cent for Ghana, 27 per cent for South Korea, 19 per cent for Malaya and 13 per cent for Thailand.

In the area of health status and services, another important contributor to productivity, in 1960 life expectancy in Ghana was 44 years as contrasted with 54 in South Korea, 53 in Malaya and 52 in Thailand. While one doctor looked after nearly 22,000 persons in Ghana, the figures per doctor were 3,540 in South Korea, 7,020 in Malaya and 7,950 in Thailand.[63]

Again we know that infrastructure is crucial to both agriculture and industry. A recent survey established that in Ghana today as much as 60 per cent of the cost of agricultural products is made up of transportation expenses. In this crucial area also a number of the Asian Tigers enjoyed untypical advantages. For example, Thailand inherited a very complex network of rural roads developed by the United States of America for security purposes. This proved very important to that country's agricultural diversification and industrialization also. South Korea and Taiwan also received massive aid from the U.S.A. for security and political reasons. Other issues can be raised. But without in any way belittling the achievement of the South East Asian countries, the point has to be made that, despite superficial appearances, they did not start their post independence history on exactly the same terms as the rest of Asia and Africa.

I wish to conclude this lecture by quoting parts of a presentation made by Chief Emeka Anyaoku, Secretary-General of the Commonwealth in B.B.C. Channel 4 Television on 9th April, 1992.

> The socio-economic achievements of independent Africa tend to be overlooked in the interest of sensational reporting. The extent of the achievements can be seen by comparing the position at independence with the position in subsequent years using the usual indicators of the quality of life.

He went on to identify increased literacy, public health delivery, decrease in infant mortality rates etc.

> Even in the more difficult area of economic growth, there have been notable advances. Between 1961 and 1973, that is before the outbreak of the oil crises, a number of African countries experienced an average annual growth rate of over four per cent. These included Malawi, Kenya, Lesotho, Côte d'Ivoire, the Congo and Gabon. A few averaged even higher rates. For most African countries this period of economic buoyancy came to a close at the end of the 1970s and was followed soon after the beginning of the 1980's by a crisis which continues to this day. Rising prices of oil and manufactured imports, the continuing falling of commodity prices, and not least, mistaken policies in the past are the principal reasons for Africa's economic crises.[64]

Similar views were stated in the editorial of *West Africa*, the weekly journal based in London, in the issue of 27th April, 1992. It said, in the 30 years of independence. Africa has recorded impressive achievement in education, medicine, child care and infrastructural development. Three decades of independence have definitely given the African people several times more in terms of socio-economic development than centuries of colonial rule ever did.

Furthermore, the economic straits in which African countries find themselves is directly related to unfair trade practices in which they are short changed by their trading partners in the north.[65]

Mr. Chairman, Ladies and Gentlemen, in conclusion, we should reject the insidious insinuation that the post colonial history of Africa has been one of unredeemed gloom.

As the tortoise explains — it dances just as vigorously as possible, it is because of its hard shell that the intricate moves it makes are not immediately observable. Thank you for your attention.

REFERENCES

1. Young, Crawford, 1985. "African Relations with the Major Powers" in Carter, G. M. and Patrick O'meara (eds). *African Independence: The first twenty-five years,* p.219, Indiana University Press, Bloomington.
2. American Academy of Arts and Sciences, 1982. *Daedalus,* Spring.
3. Carter, G. M. and Patrick O'meara, 1985, (eds). *Op. cit.*
4. Rimmer, Douglas (ed.), 1991. *Africa 30 years on: The Record and Outlook After Thirty years of Independence.* Examined for the Royal African Society, London.
5. Calvocoressi, Peter, 1985. *Independent Africa and the World,* p.1, Longman, London.
6. Jackson, R. H. and Rosberg, C. G. 1985. "The Marginality of African States" in Carter, G. M. and Patrick O'meara (eds.), *op. cit.* p.47.
7. *Ibid*
8. Carter, G. M. and Patrick O'meara (eds.), 1985, *op. cit.;* p.ix.
9. Lofchie, M. F., 1985. "Africa's Agrarian Malaise" in *ibid..*
10. Lipset, S. M., 1963. *The First New Nation. The U.S. in Historical and Comparative Perspective,* Basic Books Inc., New York.
11. Buah, F. K., 1980. *A History of Ghana,* Macmillan Education Ltd., London, p.184.
12. *The Constitution of the Republic of Ghana, 1960,* Part X, Article 55(1). See, Austin, D. 1970, *Politics in Ghana,* 1946–1960, Oxford University Press, London, p.446.

13. Buah, F. K. *op. cit*, pp.183–185.
14. Austin, Dennis. 1962 "Strong Rule in Ghana", *The Listener*, 67, p.66.
15. *Ibid.*
16. Buah, *op. cit.*
17. Boahen, A. A., 1989. *The Ghanaian Sphinx: Reflections on the contemporary history of Ghana 1972–87*. The J. B. Danquah Memorial Lectures 21st Series, February, 1988. Ghana Academy of Science, Accra, p.37.
18. Lipset, S. M., *op. cit.*, p.91.
19. *Ibid.*
20. Smith, J. M., 1956. *Freedom Fetters. The Alien and Sedition Laws and American Civil Liberties*. Cornell University Press, Ithaca, New York, p.22.
21. *Ibid.*, p.424.
22. Lipset, S. M., *op. cit.*, p.40.
23. Bassett, J. S., 1960. *The Federalist System*. Harper and Bros. New York, pp.263–264.
24. Hofstadter, R., W. Miller and D. Aaron, 1959. *The American Republic*, Englewood Cliffs. New Jersey, pp.331–332.
25. Chambers, W. N., 1963. *Political Parties in a New Nation: The American Experience 1776–1809*, Oxford University Press, New York, p.173.
26. Levy, Leonard W., 1960. *Legacy of Suppression: Freedom of Speech and Press in Early American History*. Cambridge University Press, Cambridge, pp.302–305.
27. Lipset, S. M., *op. cit.*, p.43.
28. Hook, S., P. Kurtz, and M. Todorovich (eds.), 1974. *The Idea of a Modern University*, Prometheus Books, Buffalo, New York, p.69.
29. *Ibid.*, p.16.
30. *Ibid.*, p.18.
31. *Ibid.*, p.19.
32. *Ibid.*, p.11.
33. Cunliffe, M., 1959. *The Nation Takes Shape*. University of Chicago Press, Chicago, p.181.
34. Lipset, S. M., *op. cit.*, p.15.
35. Chambers, W. N., *op. cit.*, p.96.
36. Lipset, S. M., *op. cit.*, p.35.
37. Howard, Rhoda. *Colonialism and Underdevelopment in Ghana*, Croom Helm, London, 1978, p.233.
38. Calvocoressi, Peter, *op. cit.*, p.144.
39. Lipset, S. M., *op. cit.*, p.46.
40. *Ibid.*, p.48.
41. Norton, M. B., D. M. Katzman, P. D. Escott, *et al* (eds.), 1982. *A People and a Nation: A History of the United States*, Vol.I to 1877, Houghton Mifflin Co., Boston, p.222.
42. Lipset, S. M., *op. cit.*, p.48.

43. Cunliffe, M., *op. cit.*, 111.
44. Lipset, S. M., *op. cit.*, p.50.
45. *Ibid.*, p.54.
46. Young, Crawford, *op. cit.*, p.220.
47. Calvocoressi, Peter, *op. cit.*, p.95.
48. Leys, C. 1982. "African Economic Development: Theory and Practice" in *Daedalus*, *op. cit.*, 106.
49. Lipset, S. M., *op. cit.*, p.63.
50. Norton, Katzman, *et al.*, *op. cit.*, 181.
51. Thompson, W. S., 1969. *Ghana's Foreign Policy 1957–66.* Princeton University Press, Princeton, New Jersey, p.445, Appendix; passim.
52. Lipset, S. M., *op. cit.*, p.91.
53. Kennedy, P. 1979. "Indigenous Capitalism in Ghana", Review of *African Political Economy.* Vol. 8 Jan-April 1979, p.29.
54. Current, R. N., T. H. William, and F. Friedel, 1966, *American History: A Survey,* Alfred A. Knopf, New York, p.155.
55. *Ibid.*, p.157.
56. Buah, F. K. *A History of Ghana, op. cit.*, 178–178 and Mc William, H. O. A. and M. A. Kwamena-Poh, 1975. *The Development of Education in Ghana,* Third Edition London, Longmans, pp.116–129.
57. Shannon, F. A., 1951. *America's Economic Growth,* Macmillan Education Ltd., London, pp.251–252.
58. Baydo, G. K., 1974. *A Topical History of the United States,* Prentice Hall, Englewood Cliffs, p.371.
59. *Ibid.*, p.369.
60. Hutchful Ebo, 1987. "The Development of the Army Officer-Corps in Ghana 1956–1968" *UNIVERSITAS.* An Inter-Faculty Journal of the University of Ghana, Legon Vol.9, pp.32–35.
61. Lipset, S. M., *op. cit.*, p.93.
62. Jacobs, J. R., 1947. *The Beginning of the U.S. Army 1783–1812.* Princeton, New Jersey University Press, cited in Lipset, *op. cit.*, p.93.
63. Ampem II, Nana Wereko, 1994. *Ghana's Economic Progress: The Dreams, the Realities and the prospect.* The 4th Accra Academy Foundation Lectures, Accra Academy, Accra, p.9.
64. Anyaoku Chief, E. Presentation for B.B.C. Channel 4, Television Programme "Opinions" on 9th April, 1992, excerpted in *West Africa* 27th April – 3rd May, 1992, pp.7, 8, 9, 20.
65. Editorial *West Africa* 27th April – 3rd May, 1992, p.705.

www.ingramcontent.com/pod-product-compliance
Lightning Source LLC
Chambersburg PA
CBHW021813220426
43662CB00006B/303